BEBOP SCALES
JAZZ SCALES AND PATTERNS IN ALL 12 KEYS

by JOE RIPOSO

Published by
JAMEY AEBERSOLD JAZZ®
P.O. Box 1244
New Albany, IN 47151-1244
www.jazzbooks.com
ISBN 978-1-56224-037-0

Engraving by JOE RIPOSO
Engraving Formatting and Editing by KATIE COSTELLO & JASON A. LINDSEY
Cover Design & Layout by JASON A. LINDSEY

Table of Contents

Use of Chromatic Tones

For the following two reasons an added chromatic tone should be used when playing eight-note scale patterns.

1. Adding a chromatic note to the eight-note scale will allow for better phrase balance.

2. The added chromatic note will allow for the chord tones of the scale to fall on a strong down beat in the measure

Compare the following examples:

A.

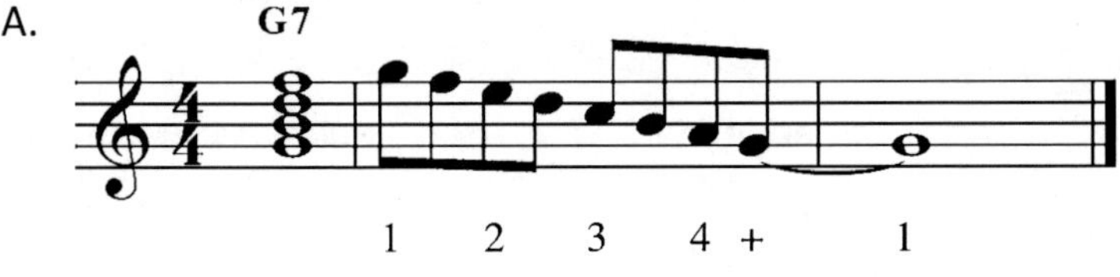

B.

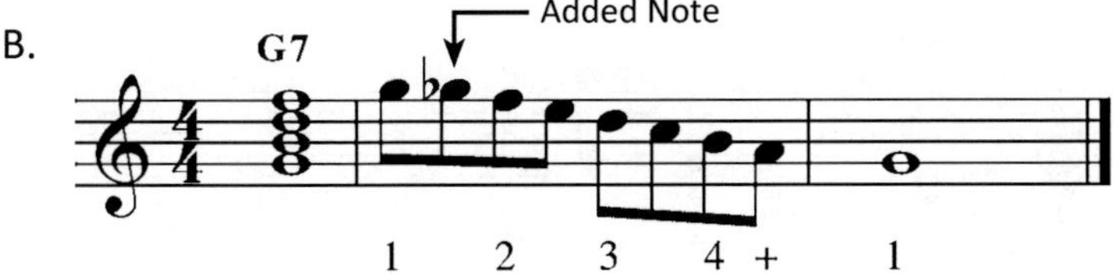

In Example (A) the last note "G" falls on the "and" of the 4th beat of the measure. This makes the scale sound awkward. The first note "G" falls on the 1st beat, which is a chord tone, but on all the other beats (2, 3, and 4) a non-basic chord tone appears.

In example (B), the last note "G" falls on the 1st beat of the second measure, which gives the phrase proper musical balance. The addition of the chromatic half step in the eight note scale in example (B) solved the problem of not having a chord tone fall on all the down beats. The note "G" is on the 1st beat, the note "F" is now on the 2nd beat, the note "D" falls on the 3rd beat, "B" falls on the 4th beat, and the note "G" falls on the 1st beat of the next measure giving the scale balance.

The chromatic ½ step should be used in all eighth-note scales. You will find that the ½ step will appear between two different notes in each scale.

In the Major scale, the chromatic ½ step is used between the 5th and 6th scale tone while in the Dorian scale the chromatic ½ step is used between the 3rd and 4th note of the scale. In the Mixolydian or Dominant scale, the chromatic ½ step is used between the 7th and 8th note of the scale and in the Locrian or half diminished scale the chromatic ½ step is used between the 5th and 6th note of the scale.

To develop our ear to hear and become comfortable using the added chromatic ½ steps in each of these scales, play them slowly at first. Careful listening while playing these scales will help to develop your ear to hear where the chromatic ½ steps fall in the different scales.

MAJOR SCALE
In the Major scale, the added ½ step is used between the 5th and 6th scale step.

1, 2, 3, 4, (5, #5, 6), 7, 8

DORIAN SCALE
In the Dorian scale, the added ½ step is used between the 3rd and 4th scale step.

1, 2, (3, #3, 4,) 5, 6, 7, 8

MIXOLYDIAN (DOMINANT 7th) SCALE
In the Mixoldian scale, the added ½ step is used between the 7th and 8th
scale step.

1, 2, 3, 4, 5, 6, (7, #7, 8)

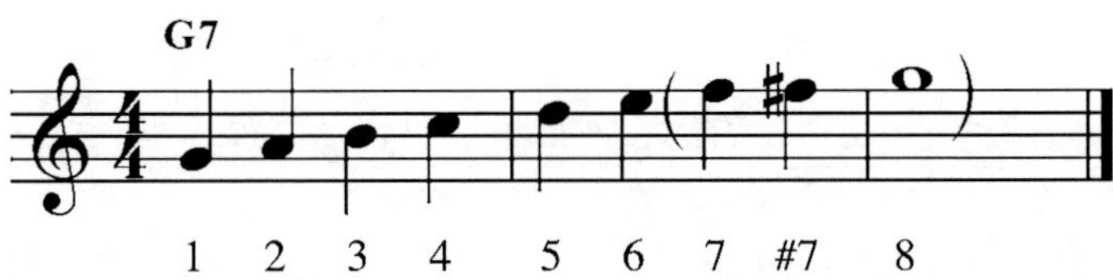

HALF-DIMINISHED SCALE (Locrian)
In the Half-Diminished scale, the chromatic ½ step is used between the
5th and 6th note of the scale.

1, 2, 3, 4, (5, #5, 6,) 7, 8

NOTES

____

____

____

____

____

____

____

____

____

____

Major Scales

With the added ½ Step in a Chromatic Pattern

Notice Ex.1A in the incorrect playing of the C Major eight-note scale, the note "C" is on the first beat of the measure which is a chord tone. Now look at the 2nd beat, we have the note "A" which is not a chord tone. On the 3rd beat of the measure, we have the note "F" which is not a chord tone and is what is called an avoidance tone. This note should not be played on a strong beat. Another non chordal tone "D" falls on the 4th beat.

The additional problem we create is that the resolution falls on the "up" beat of 4, thus creating an unbalanced scale line.

By comparison, look at Ex. 1B the correct playing of the C Major eight-note scale. The resolution or home tone "C" falls on the downbeat which gives the scale the proper balance. You now have created a scale with all the basic chord tones on each down beat of the measure. The 3rd of the chord, which is the most important note of a chord, now falls on the 4th beat of the measure.

Play the following Major scales to develop your ear to hear the added chromatic tone. Learn to play these scales without reading them from the printed page.

D Maj7
E♭ Maj7
E Maj7
F Maj7
F♯ Maj7
G Maj7
A♭ Maj7
A Maj7
B♭ Maj7
B Maj7

Major Scales

With the added ½ Step in a Scale Pattern in 4ths

Using the same concept as in the chromatic pattern, the following is an ascending root pattern in 4ths. Many jazz tunes use the chord progression of a 4th, often called the "cycle." This is true especially in the middle section of a tune called the bridge.

By practicing this exercise, you will develop your ear to hear the standard progression of a 4th and how the appropriate scale with the ½ step is used.

Play the following 12 scale progressions with and without the printed page. This is all about loading up with the sounds necessary to play over a progression in 4ths.

C#Maj7
F#Maj7
B Maj7
E Maj7
A Maj7
D Maj7
G Maj7

Major Scales

With the added ½ Step Ascending and Descending Pattern in Major 3rds

To continue to load up with your experience of playing scales with the added ½ step over some of the most common chord progressions, you need to practice the following:

Many chord progressions use the interval of a Major 3rd.

Play the following 12 scale progressions with and without the printed page. This is all about loading up with the sounds necessary to play over a progression in Major 3rds.

A Maj7
D Maj7
F#Maj7
Bb Maj7
Eb Maj7
G Maj7
B Maj7

Major Scales

With the added ½ Step Ascending and Descending Pattern in Minor 3rds

To continue to load up with your experience of playing scales with the added ½ step over some of the most common chord progressions, you need to practice the following:

Many chord progressions use the interval of a Minor 3rd.

Play the following 12 scale progressions with and without the printed page. This is all about loading up with the sounds necessary to play over a root progression in Minor 3rds.

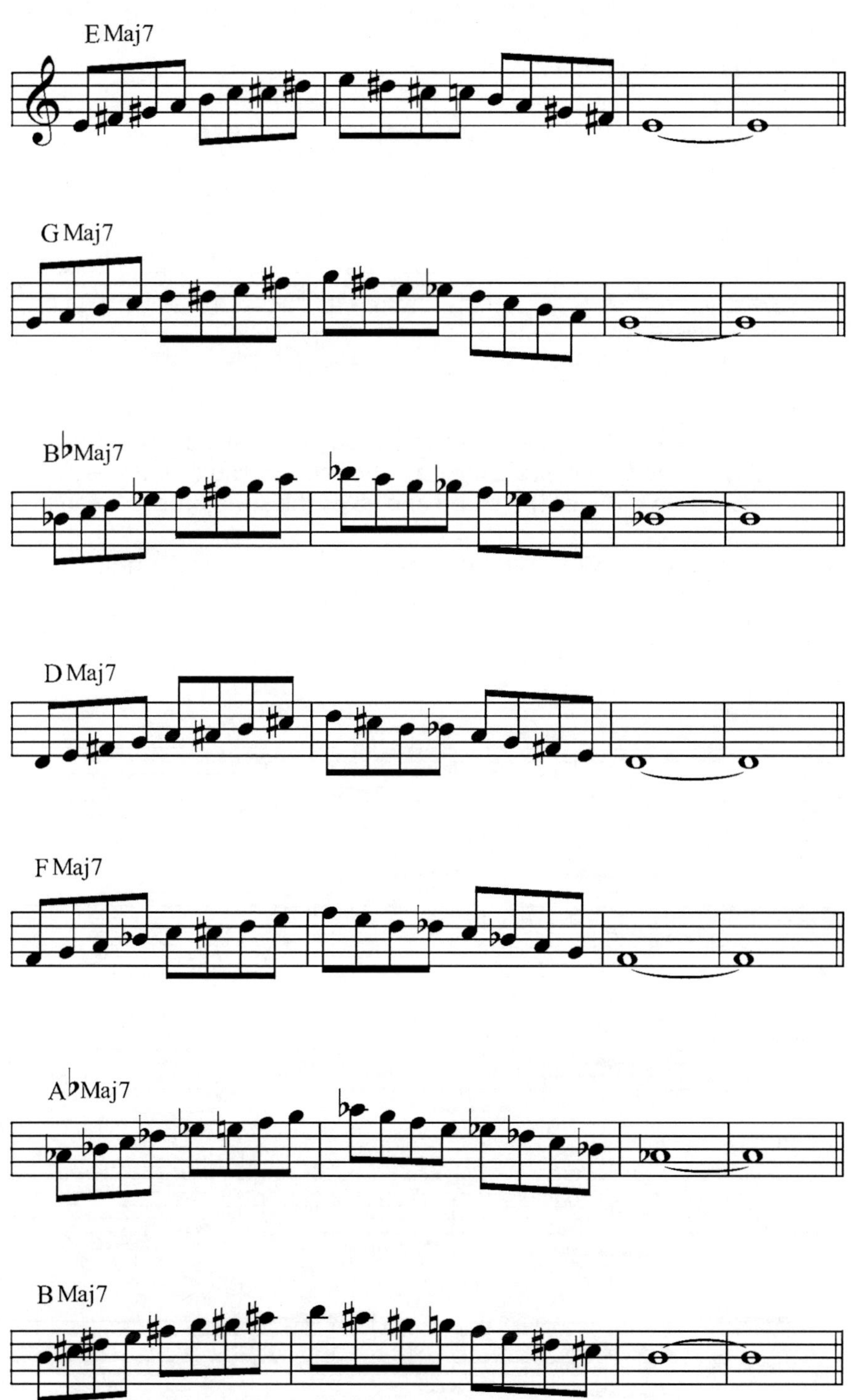

E Maj7
G Maj7
B♭Maj7
D Maj7
F Maj7
A♭Maj7
B Maj7

Dorian Scales

With the added ½ Step in a Chromatic Pattern

2A (Incorrect) 2B (Correct)

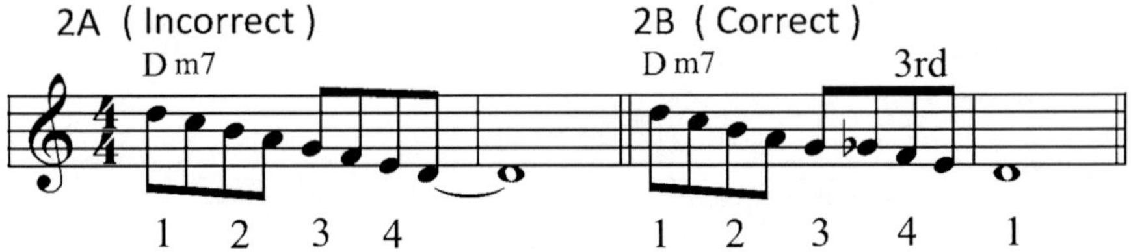

In a Dorian scale, all the notes sound good. There are no wrong notes when playing the Dorian scale over a minor chord. The use of the ½ step in a Dorian scale outlines the chord and gives the scale proper balance.

In example labeled correct (2B), the chord tones fall on each primary beat of the measure. Please note that the 3rd of the chord falls on the 4th beat of the measure.

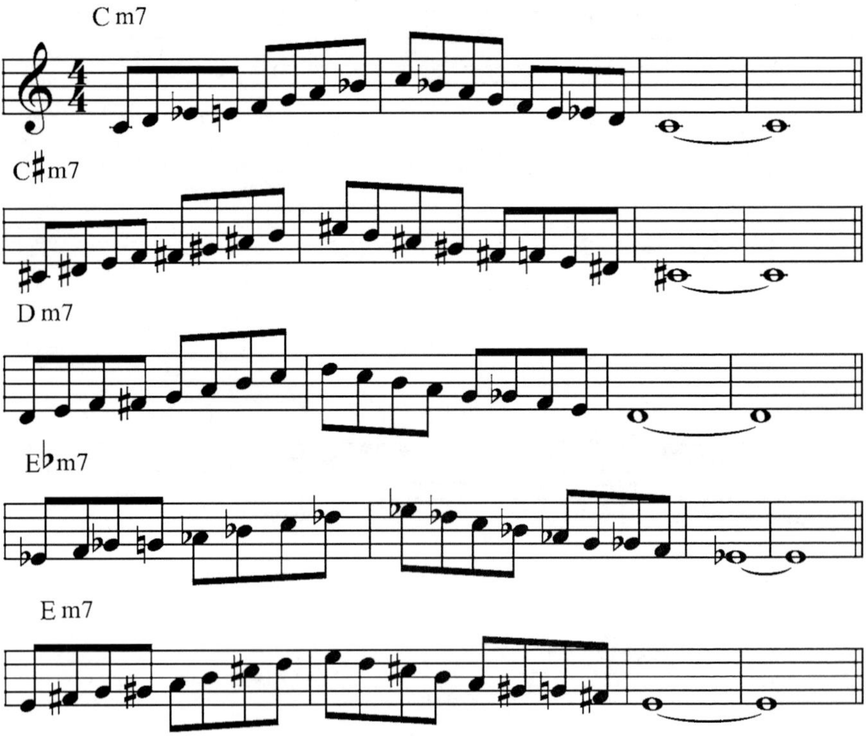

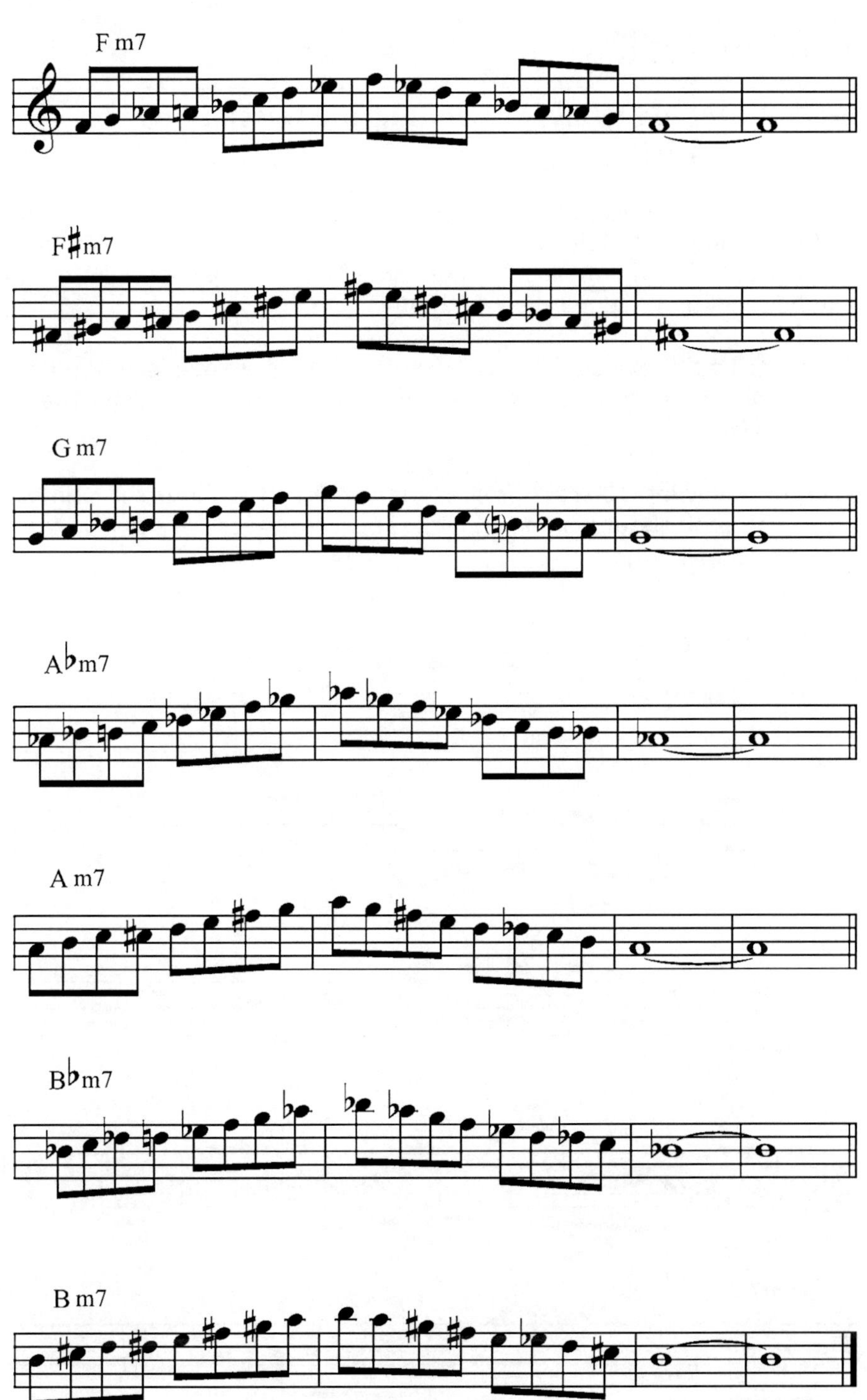

F m7
F#m7
G m7
Ab m7
A m7
Bb m7
B m7

Dorian Scales

With the added ½ Step Ascending and Descending Pattern in 4ths

Using the same concept as in the chromatic pattern, the following is an ascending and descending pattern in 4ths. Many jazz tunes use the chord progression of a 4th, often called the "cycle." This is true especially in the middle section of a tune called the bridge.

By practicing this exercise, you will develop your ear to hear the standard progression of a 4th and how the appropriate Dorian scale with the ½ step is used.

Play the following 12 scale progressions with and without the printed page. This is all about loading up with the sounds necessary to play over a progression in 4ths.

C#m7
F#m7
B m7
E m7
A m7
D m7
G m7

Dorian Scales

With the added ½ Step Ascending and Descending Pattern in Major 3rds

To continue to load up with your experience of playing scales with the added ½ step over some of the most common chord progressions, you need to practice the following:

Many chord progressions use the interval of a Major 3rd.

Play the following 12 scale progressions with and without the printed page. This is all about loading up with the sounds necessary to play over a progression in Major 3rds.

A m7
D m7
F#m7
Bbm7
Ebm7
G m7
B m7

Dorian Scales

With the added ½ Step Ascending and Descending Pattern in Minor 3rds

To continue to load up with your experience of playing scales with the added ½ step over some of the most common chord progressions, you need to practice the following:

Many chord progressions use the interval of a Minor 3rd.

Play the following 12 scale progressions with and without the printed page. This is all about loading up with the sounds necessary to play over a progression in Minor 3rds.

E m7
G m7
B♭m7
D m7
F m7
A♭m7
B m7

Mixolydian (Dominant 7th) Scales

With the added ½ Step in a Chromatic Pattern

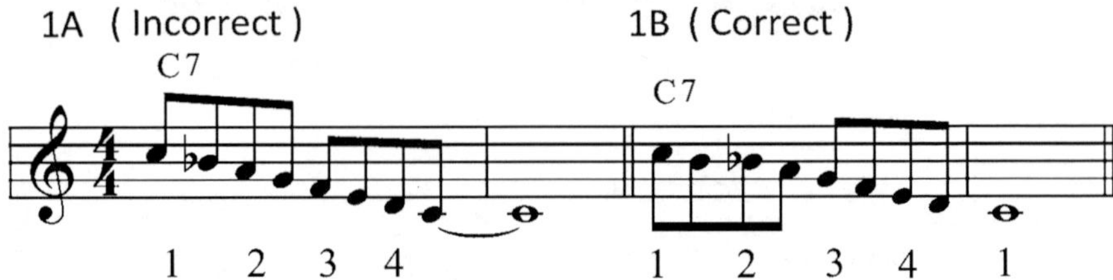

Notice Ex.1A in the incorrect playing of the C7 (dom.7) eight-note scale, the note "C" is on the first beat of the measure which is a chord tone. Now look at the 2nd beat, we have the note "A" which is not a chord tone. On the 3rd beat of the measure, we have the note "F" which is not a chord tone and is what is called an avoidance tone. This note should not be played on a strong beat.

The additional problem we create is the resolution falls on the "up" beat of 4, thus creating an unbalanced scale line.

By comparison, look at Ex. 1B the correct playing of the C7 (dom.7) scale. The resolution or home tone "C" falls on the first beat of the measure which gives the scale the proper balance. You now have created a scale with all the basic chord tones on each down beat of the measure. The 3rd of the chord, which is the most important note of a chord, now falls on the 4th beat of the measure.

Play the following Mixolydian scales to develop your ear to hear the added chromatic tone. Learn to play these scales without reading them from the printed page.

Eb7
E7
F7
F#7
G7
Ab7
A7
Bb7
B7

Mixolydian (Dominant 7th) Scales

With the added ½ Step Ascending and Descending Pattern in 4ths

Using the same concept as in the chromatic pattern, the following is an ascending and descending pattern in 4ths. Many jazz tunes use the chord progression of a 4th, often called the "cycle." This is true especially in the middle section of a tune called the bridge.

By practicing this exercise, you will develop your ear to hear the standard progression of a 4th and how the appropriate scale with the ½ step is used.

Play the following 12 scale progressions with and without the printed page. This is all about loading up with the sounds necessary to play over a progression in 4ths.

C#7
F#7
B 7
E 7
A 7
D 7
G 7

Mixolydian (Dominant 7th) Scales

With the added ½ Step Ascending and Descending Pattern in Major 3rds

To continue to load up with your experience of playing scales with the added ½ step over some of the most common chord progressions, you need to practice the following:

Many chord progressions use the interval of a Major 3rd.

Play the following 12 scale progressions with and without the printed page. This is all about loading up with the sounds necessary to play over a progression in Major 3rds.

A 7
D 7
F#7
Bb7
Eb7
G 7
B 7

Mixolydian (Dominant 7th) Scales

With the added ½ Step Ascending and Descending Pattern in Minor 3rds

To continue to load up with your experience of playing scales with the added ½ step over some of the most common chord progressions, you need to practice the following:

Many chord progressions use the interval of a Minor 3rd.

Play the following 12 scale progressions with and without the printed page. This is all about loading up with the sounds necessary to play over a progression in Minor 3rds.

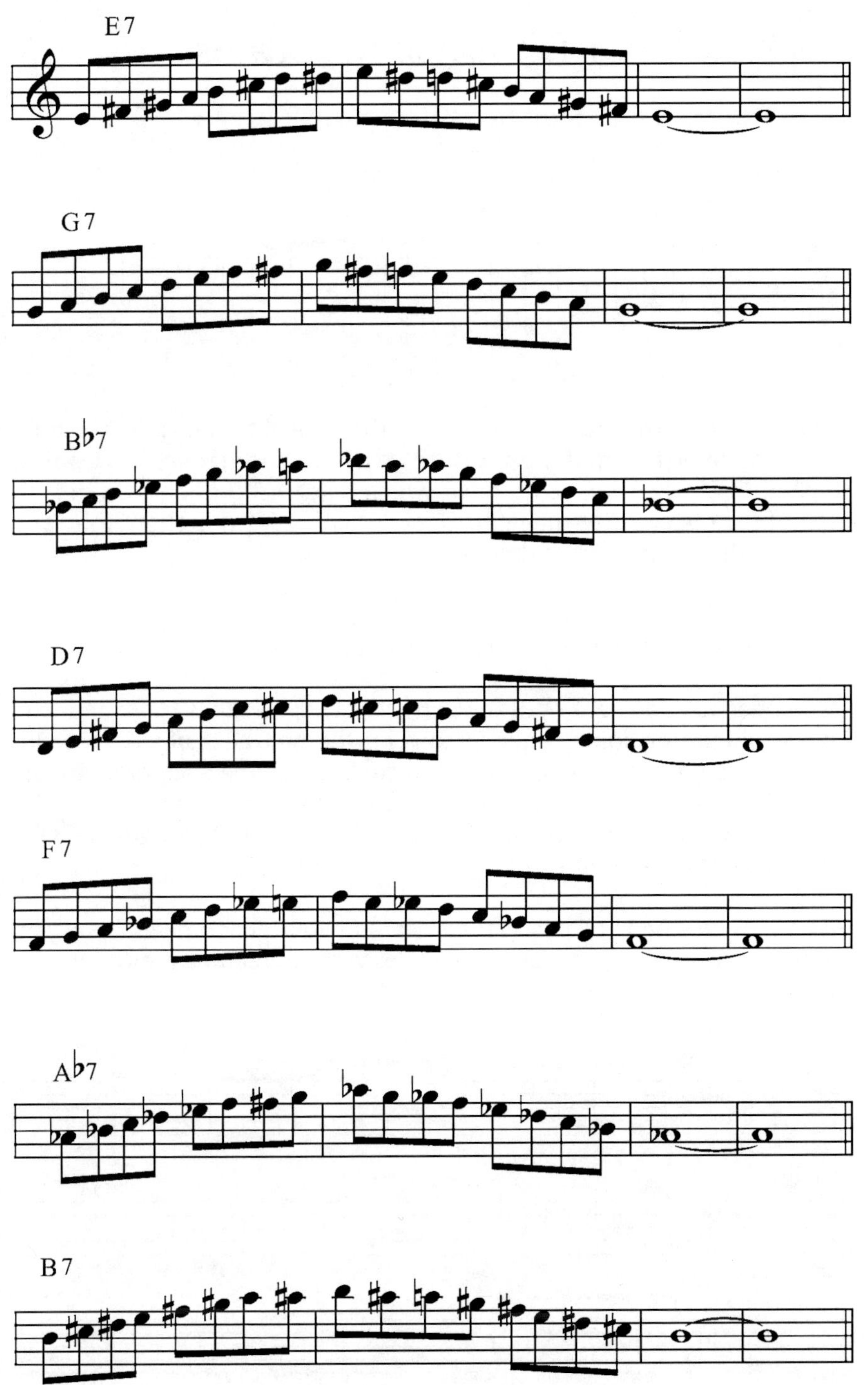

E 7
G 7
B♭7
D 7
F 7
A♭7
B 7

Locrian (Half-Diminished) Scales

With the added ½ Step in a Chromatic Pattern

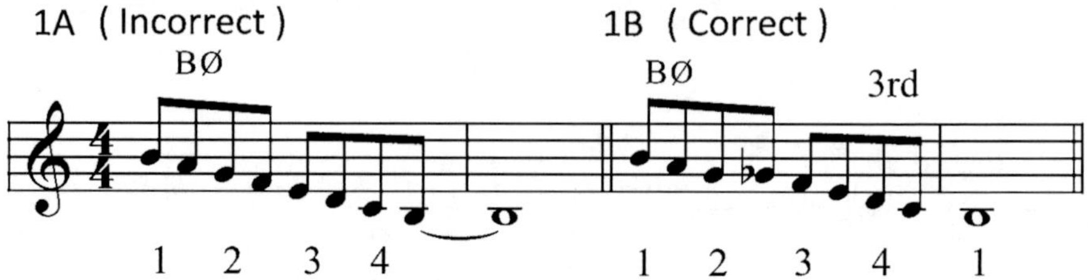

Notice Ex.1A in the incorrect playing of the BØ eight-note scale, the note "B" is on the first beat of the measure which is a chord tone. Now look at the 2nd beat, we have the note "G" which is not a chord tone. On the 3rd beat of the measure, we have the note "E" which is not a chord tone and a "C" on the 4th beat of the measure.

The additional problem we create is the resolution falls on the "up" beat of 4, thus creating an unbalanced scale line.

By comparison, look at Ex. 1B the correct playing of the BØ Locrian scale. The resolution or home tone "B" falls on the first beat of the measure which gives the scale the proper balance. You now have created a scale with all the basic chord tones on each down beat of the measure. The 3rd of the chord, which is the most important note of a chord, now falls on the 4th beat of the measure.

Play the following Locrian scales to develop your ear to hear the added chromatic tone. Learn to play these scales without reading them from the printed page.

Eb∅
E∅
F∅
F#∅
G∅
Ab∅
A∅
Bb∅
B∅

Locrian (Half-Diminished) Scales

With the added ½ Step Ascending and Descending Pattern in 4ths

Using the same concept as in the chromatic pattern, the following is an ascending and descending pattern in 4ths. Many jazz tunes use the chord progression of a 4th, often called the "cycle." This is true especially in the middle section of a tune called the bridge.

By practicing this exercise, you will develop your ear to hear the standard progression of a 4th and how the appropriate scale with the ½ step is used.

Play the following 12 scale progressions with and without the printed page. This is all about loading up with the sounds necessary to play over a progression in 4ths.

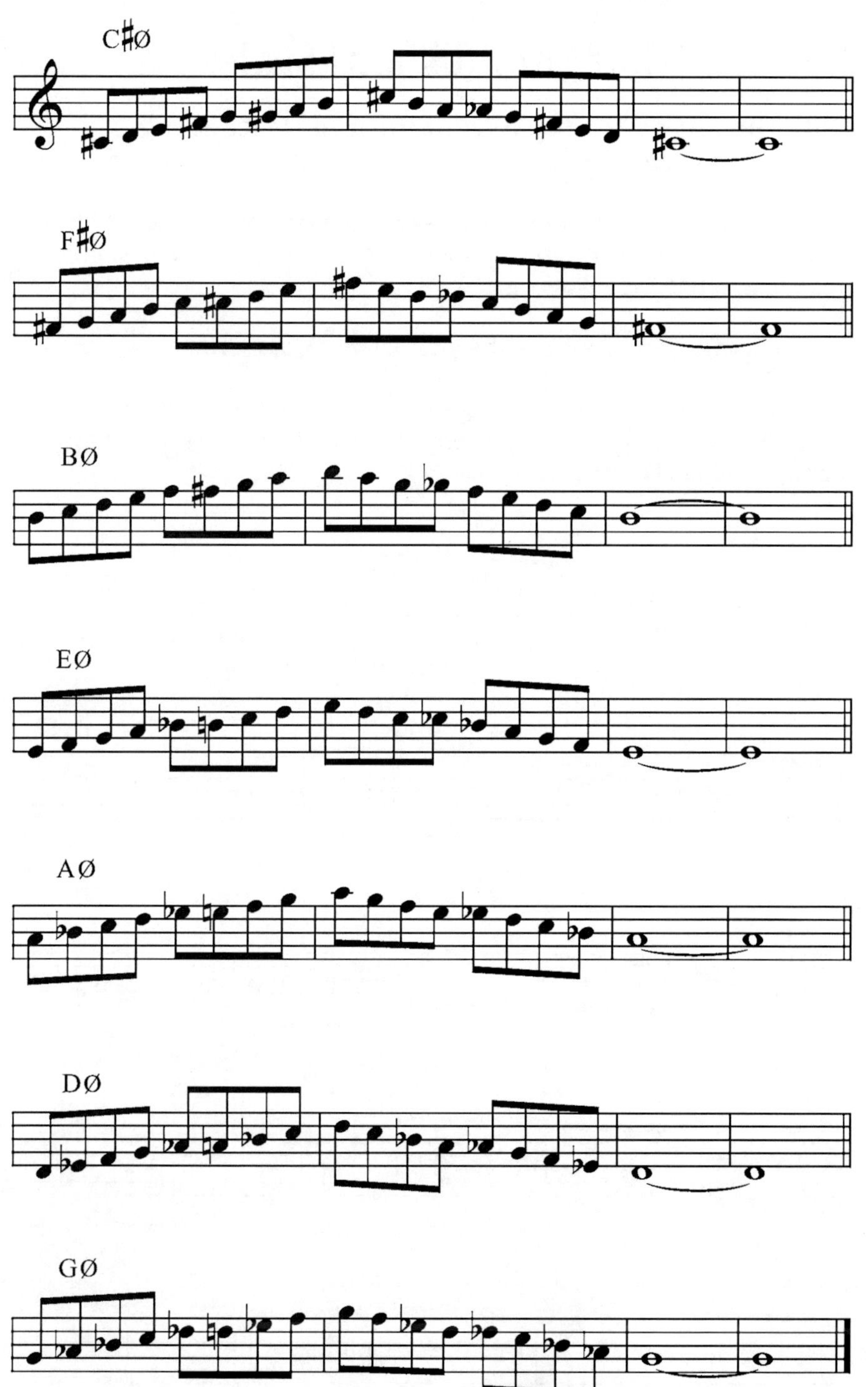
C#ø
F#ø
Bø
Eø
Aø
Dø
Gø

Locrian (Half-Diminished) Scales

With the added ½ Step Ascending and Descending Pattern in Major 3rds

To continue to load up with your experience of playing scales with the added ½ step over some of the most common chord progressions, you need to practice the following:

Many chord progressions use the interval of a Major 3rd.

Play the following 12 scale progressions with and without the printed page. This is all about loading up with the sounds necessary to play over a progression in Major 3rds.

Locrian Scales (With the added ½ Step Ascending and Descending Pattern in Major 3rds) | 35

Locrian (Half-Diminished) Scales

With the added ½ Step Ascending and Descending Pattern in Minor 3rds

To continue to load up with your experience of playing scales with the added ½ step over some of the most common chord progressions, you need to practice the following:

Many chord progressions use the interval of a Minor 3rd.

Play the following 12 scale progressions with and without the printed page. This is all about loading up with the sounds necessary to play over a progression in Minor 3rds.

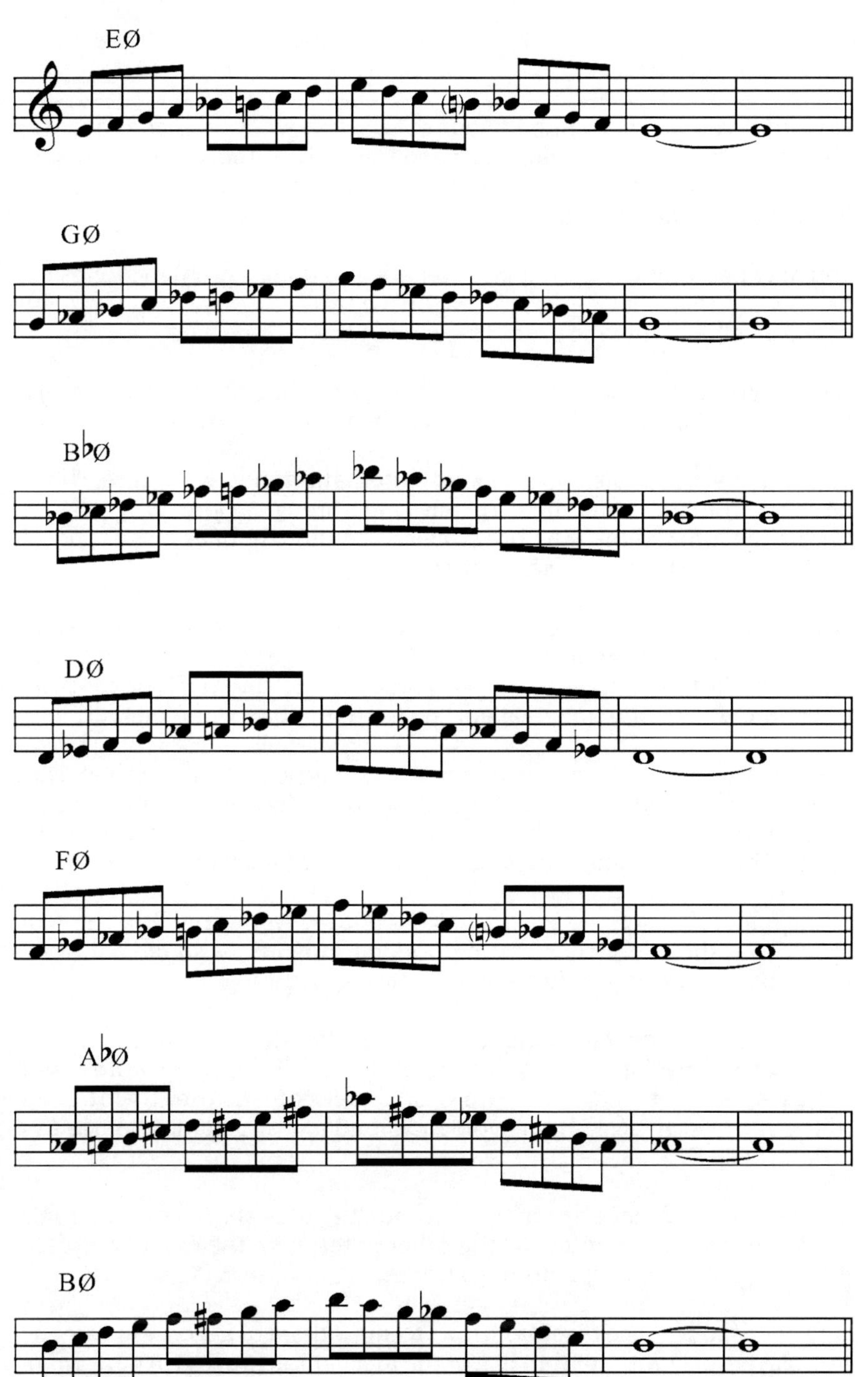

EØ
GØ
B♭Ø
DØ
FØ
A♭Ø
BØ

Application

Now that you have developed your ear to hear where the added ½ step chromatic tone can be used, you need to combine the scales to shape a melodic line. The most common use of these combined scales is over a II7, V7, I chord progression.

You may find that there are places where additional chromatic tones can be used. In the following examples, I have taken the liberty to use a few of these extra chromatic tones to even out the melodic line.

Remember, the reason for using ½ step chromatic tones is so that the chord tones fall on all the strong down beats in a measure.

Jazz players use scales with added chromatic tones with ease. These added chromatic tones help to navigate through chord progressions. Chromatic tones in the 8th note scale can be thought of as hinge tones. It is important to hinge one scale to an other.

A jazz player selects a target note in the new chord to go to and uses the added chromatic tone in the 8th note scale to get to the desired note. Using the 8th note scale in this way will provide the much needed line direction, or as some times called, "forward motion" in the melodic line.

Each chord in a progression needs to be married to each other. They should not be thought of as individual chords. They are all related to each other in the progression. Think of the key center of each chord and play on the key center using the unique color tones of each chord.

In the minor 7 chord, the 3rd is a desired note as well as the 7th. The note that makes the minor chord sound Dorian is the 6th. As stated earlier, all the notes of a Dorian scale are good notes to use.

The most common target note for better line direction in the Dom.7 chord or Mixolydian scale is the 3rd and 7th. All the other notes, with the exception of the 4th note, are good target notes to use. The 4th note of the Mixolydian scale is an avoidance tone and should not be use as a target tone.

In a Major chord, once again, the 3rd and 7th notes are the desired tones to consider as target notes. All the other notes, with the exception of the 4th note, are good target notes to use.

One needs to practice these concepts to allow them to become automatic. Jazz players play without thinking of the mechanical process of performing these concepts. They do not make a physical response when they hear a chord progression but they make a mental response.

Examples

The following pages are devoted to providing an experience of how these scales can be used. Play and analyze them to develop an understanding of why they sound like they do. Feel the "forward motion" created by this ½ step approach.

(note the added chromatic tone D# in Ex. 4.)

6.
G m7   C 7   F
4/4
7. G m7   C 7   F Maj7
8. G m7   C 7   F Maj7
9. G m7   C 7   F Maj7
10. G m7   C 7   F Maj7
11. E m7   A 7   D Maj7
12. A m7   D 7   A m7   D 7   G Maj7

20. D m7   G 7   C Maj7
21. G m7   C 7b9   F Maj7
22. G m7   C 7b9   F 6/9
23. A m7   D 7   G m7   C 7b9   F 6/9
24. E m7   A 7b9   D m7   G 7b9   C 6/9
3
25. E m   A 7b9   D m   G 7b9   C 6/9
26. A m7   D 7   A m7   D 7b9   G Maj7

Examples

Locrian (Half-Diminished) Phrases using the ½ Steps

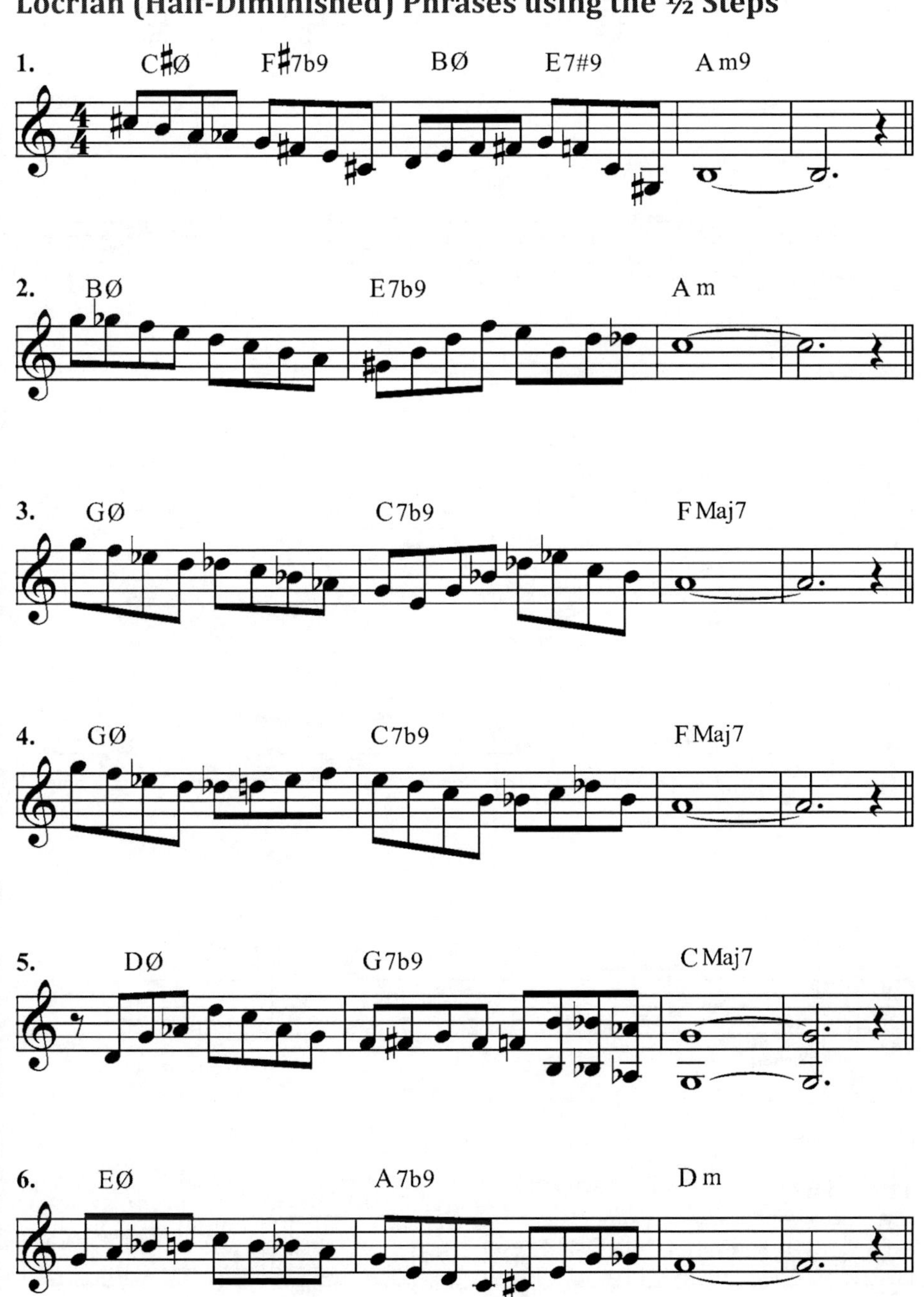

7.
F#Ø   B7#9   EØ   A7#9   Dm

8.
AØ   D7#9   Gm

9.
AØ   D7b9   Gm

10.
AØ   D7b9   Gm9

11.
EØ   A7b9   Dm

12.
DØ   G7b9   C6/9

13.
GØ   C7b9   F Maj7

14.
F#Ø   B7b9   E m6

15.
F#Ø   B7b9   E m

16.
EØ   A7b9   D m

17.
DØ   G7b9   C Maj7

18.
DØ   G7b9   C Maj7

Summary

Now that you have played all the written jazz phrases, your ear should be able to hear your own jazz phrases using ½ step chromatic tones.

As mentioned previously, these are more traditional ways to use the chromatic ½ steps but additional chromatic ½ steps can be used between other notes as well. **You need to remember the reason for using the chromatic ½ steps is so the chord tones fall on the down beat.**

The more chromatic tones used in a measure, the fewer chord tones will fall on the down beat. This will cause the phrase to have a less harmonic tonal center.

In order to become proficient at using these chromatic ½ steps in your phrases, you need to practice until it becomes an automatic response and not a technique that you have to think about to manufacture a jazz phrase.

Experience is your best teacher so improvise using this concept as often as you can. Each time, try the notes and ½ steps in a different order and over different chord progressions.

As stated in the beginning of this book, there are two basic reasons for using the chromatic ½ step when playing eight-note scale patterns:

1. Adding a chromatic ½ step when playing a eight-note phrase will allow for better phrase balance.

2. The added chromatic ½ step will allow for the chord tones in the scale or phrases to fall on a strong down beat in the measure.

About the Author

JOE RIPOSO (Saxophonist, Composer, Arranger and Jazz Educator) is the Director of Jazz Studies at Syracuse University. The former Director of Music Education for the Liverpool Central School District (31 years) served as past president of the International Association of Jazz Educators (N.Y.S. Unit) and as the North Eastern Division Coordinator for the International Association of Jazz Educators.

Riposo has served as Jazz Coordinator and Clinician for the NY State School Music Association. He is the recipient of the presidential medallion for his leadership and contributions to the New York State School Music Association. Riposo holds the New York State School Music Association certification as a Woodwind Adjudicator and as a State Jazz Adjudicator.

Riposo is also an active performer, having worked in house bands for nationally known artists such as Tony Bennett, Sammy Davis, Jr., Nat King Cole, Ella Fitzgerald and the McGuire Sisters, and others. He has played a special performance with the Woody Herman Band on tour with Jackie Leonard and Tony Bennett. He has also performed in bands for Diane Schuur, Harry Connick Jr. and Natalie Cole. Riposo also conducted jazz ensembles with many renowned guest soloists including Dizzy Gillespie, Phil Woods, Marvin Stamm, Glenn Drewes, Darius Brubeck, Nick Brignola, and Bob Kindred. Riposo appears frequently as clinician, adjudicator, guest conductor and soloist in many jazz festivals throughout the U.S.

He is the composer of numerous published compositions and is the author of *Jazz Improvisation "The Whole-Brain Approach"* and a Recorder Method (1999 by LMI) and a second Recorder Method published by Increase Music. Joe is a contracted writer for Increase Music Publishers, Walrus Music Publishers and Jamey Aebersold Jazz®.

Riposo received the Outstanding Jazz Educators Award from the National Band Association for effective leadership in instrumental music education by developing successful concert and jazz bands in America's schools.

On November 21, 1997, Riposo was inducted into the (SAMMYS) Music Hall of Fame. He was also inducted in the Fine Arts Hall of Fame on June 8, 2003. Riposo is the recipient of the 2008 Jazz Educator of the Year Award presented by CYN Jazz Arts.

More Jazz Improv!

Patterns For Improvisation
by Oliver Nelson

One of the world's most popular patterns books, many jazz greats have fond memories of practicing from this book! An exhaustive collection of improvisational jazz patterns in various meters and feels. Comments and suggestions by the author.

Intervalic Improvisation
By Walt Weiskopf

Recording artist and master improviser, Walt Weiskopf, presents a simple technique of using only two triads to create long, exciting phrases. Recommended for intermediate or advanced players who are looking for something to help take them to the next level.

Keys Unlocked!
By Jerry Coker

Playing in all 12 keys is one of the most important skills an improviser can master. Book contains clear and concise explanations, examples, and exercises. Along the way, Jerry shares his musical journey on the way to 12 key mastery. Move to a higher level of improvisation and confidence in any musical situation.

How To Approach Standards Chromatically
By David Liebman

Clearly demonstrates superimposing chords chromatically over "standard" chord changes to play contemporary jazz lines. Includes standard and superimposed harmony for *Girl From Ipanema, Donna Lee, Autumn Leaves, Take The A Train, Satin Doll, Rhythm and Blues Changes, Impressions, India, Loft Dance, and A Love Supreme.*

The Creative Nudge
By Jerry Coker

Why do musicians choose jazz improv as an outlet for creativity? Why are we creating this music and who are we creating it for? All you need is a little information. Master jazz educator Jerry Coker has put together this wonderfully structured text summarizing topics regarding jazz and jazz improvisation; giving us all that much needed "nudge."

Available from your favorite music source or visit www.jazzbooks.com